Genre Fiction

 Essential Question
How do people get along?

Rainy Day

by Jerome Anderson

illustrated by Marcy Tippmann

"It's raining!" Jenna **moaned**.
"Now the day won't be fun.
Rain is so boring."

Jenna's cousin Nikki was coming over. They had planned to play at the park.

Rain **drummed** on the roof. "And it's noisy!" Jenna shouted.

"The rain is not boring and noisy," Gran said. "Sounds like someone got up on the wrong side of the bed."

"Did not!" said Jenna.

Gran looked **amused**. "You and Nikki can make other plans. Use your **imagination**."

STOP AND CHECK

How does Jenna feel about the rain?

The doorbell rang. It was Aunt Susan and Nikki. Nikki was wearing rain boots.

"Look! See the yellow ducks?"
Nikki asked. "I've been so **patient**.
I've waited for months to wear
these new boots!"

"The rain is **awful**." said Jenna.
"I want it to be sunny so we can
go to the park."

"Maybe the sun will come out later," Aunt Susan said. "I'm sure you can stay **entertained** until then."

Jenna sat on the couch and
pouted.

"I know you're unhappy about
the park," said Gran. "But you
can still have a good time."

Jenna knew Gran was right.

Nikki said, "I like the rain, but I'm sorry you're sad."

STOP AND CHECK

Why does Jenna pout?

"I'm okay," Jenna said. "Do you still want to go out? I can get my boots."

"Sure!" Nikki said. "And then we can have an **inside** picnic!"

"An inside picnic?" Jenna asked.

Nikki said, "We can put a blanket on the floor. Then we can eat lunch on it. We won't get wet!"

"That sounds fun," Jenna agreed.
"Gran!" she called. "We're going
outside. Then we'll make lunch."

Gran said, "Yes! That's how to **cooperate**. I'll get everything ready."

"This rainy day is not so bad after all!" said Jenna.

STOP AND CHECK

What is the new plan?

Respond to Reading

Summarize

Summarize *Rainy Day*. The Chart may help you.

Character	Clue	Point of View

Text Evidence

1. How does each girl feel about the rain at first?

   Point of View

2. Reread page 2. What does *boring* mean? What words help you to know? Vocabulary

3. How does Jenna's point of view about the rain change?

   Write About Reading

Compare Texts
Read about a group that helps kids learn and grow.

Boys & Girls Clubs

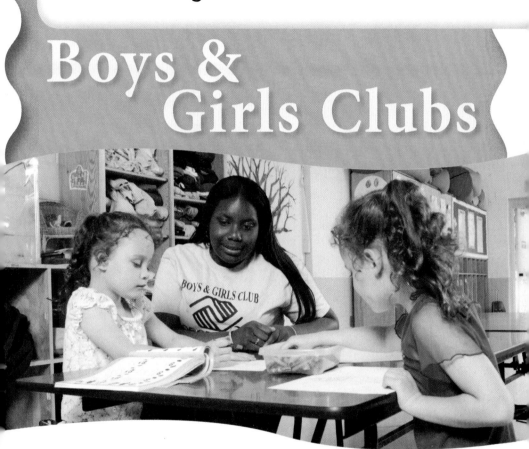

There are Boys & Girls Clubs all over the United States. What do kids do there? They play and learn.

Working together is a big part of Boys & Girls Clubs.

Kids of all ages come to the clubs. They make new friends. They learn new things.

Having fun outside is part of the clubs, too.

At the clubs, kids also play sports and do art. They learn to be good citizens. The clubs help kids to be their best!

Make Connections

What do the clubs teach kids about getting along? Essential Question

How do both stories show people getting along? Text to Text

Focus on
Social Studies

Purpose To find out why people should get along

What to Do

Step 1 ▶ Work with a partner. Talk about why getting along is important. What is something your school does to help people get along?

Step 2 ▶ Draw a picture of people at your school getting along. Share the picture with the class.